Disclaimer

Cross country skiing, whether on a groomed and trackset trail or far back in the wilderness, is potentially dangerous. Cold weather and exposure, falls, river crossings, avalanches and the possibility of losing one's way are only some of the very real dangers that must be accepted and dealt with if one is to venture onto these mountain trails. For many of us the existence of the dangers forms an integral part of the attraction of this activity.

Hopefully, this guidebook will provide information to help make your time in the mountains a safe and enjoyable experience. However, it is only a book—another tool to help you along the way. You must still learn all the techniques and skills required to venture safely into the backcountry, and you must still learn to show good judgement in applying all of these techniques. Furthermore, due to continually changing conditions and weather, the information presented in this book provides only a limited part of the overall picture. It is up to you to collect all the information necessary to make intelligent and safe decisions. This guidebook is not a substitute for experience and good judgement.

nordic trails
backcountry tours
destination slopes

Radium Ski & Snowboarding Guide

**Ted Johnson &
Chris Hofstetter**

Rocky
Mountain Books

Published by Rocky Mountain Books
#4 Spruce Centre SW, Calgary, AB T3C 3B3
Printed and bound in Canada by
RMB Kromar Printing Ltd., Winnipeg.

National Library of Canada Cataloguing in Publication Data

Johnson, Ted, 1973-
  Radium ski & snowboarding guide / Ted Johnson & Chris Hofstetter.

ISBN 0-921102-95-X

  1. Skis and skiing--British Columbia--Radium Hot Springs
Region--Guidebooks. 2. Snoeboarding--British Columbia--Radium Hot
Springs Region--Guidebooks. 3. Radium Hot Springs Region
(B.C.)--Guidebooks. I. Hofstetter, Chris, 1973-
II. Title.
GV854.8.C3J63 2003   796.93'09711'65   C2002-911516-7

CONTENTS

Information

Introduction – 6
Radium – 7
Skiing in the Radium Area – 8
Avalanches – 10
Expeditions – 11

Equipment – 12
Snowmobiles – 13
Area Map – 14
About the Authors – 87
Useful Phone Numbers – 88

Skiing Areas

Nordic Centres
Beckie Scott Nordic Centre at
Panorama Mountain Village – 16
Baptiste Lake Nordic Trails – 18
Nipika Touring Centre – 19

Purcell Tours & Destination Slopes
The Bugaboos – 22
Bugaboo Park – 23
Silver Basin – 25
Rocky Point – 27
Forster Creek – 30
Welsh Lakes – 31
Forester Basin – 33
Upper Forester – 37
Horsethief Creek – 41
McDonald Creek – 42
Farnham Creek – 43
Lake of the Hanging Glacier – 45
Toby Creek – 47
Paradise Bowl – 48
Delphine Creek & Glades – 50
Thunderbird Mine – 52
Upper Toby Creek – 53
Jumbo Creek – 54
Jumbo Pass – 56
Jumbo Glacier – 59
Jumbo Poaches – 61

Brewer Creek – 62
Coffee Pot – 63
Brewer Bowls – 64

Rockies Tours & Destination Slopes
Madias Creek – 67
The Pedley Bowls – 69
Mount Swansea – 71
Kootenay National Park – 72
Kindersley Pass – 73
West Kootenay – 75
East Kootenay – 75
Hector George – 76
Dolly Varden – 77

Backcountryt Huts, Cabins and Lodges
Conrad Kain Hut – 80
Forester Snowmobile Cabin – 81
Dave Whyte Hut – 82
Olive Hut – 83
Paradise Snowmobile Cabin – 84
Jumbo Pass Cabin – 85
Nipika Lodge – 86

INTRODUCTION

Bordered by the rugged Purcell and the majestic Rocky Mountains, Radium is quietly becoming a centre for backcountry skiers and snowboarders. The Radium area offers a wide assortment of skiing: From nordic centres and backcountry day trips to overnight glacier expeditions. It's this diversity, as well as its remoteness and uncrowded mountains, that give this area its charm.

For this book we have selected areas to ski based on their relative ease of access quality of snowpack and proximity to the town of Radium.

There are several areas we have chosen not to write about due to their lack of snowpack, difficulty of access, limited skiing potential or unjustified dangers. There are a few areas that we feel are suited to multi-day expeditions; areas that are so special that to tell you about them in detail would detract from the challenges that these tours have to offer. They are all in remote and hard to reach places and involve glacier travel, big mountain terrain, multiday logistics, a reliable snowpack and fantastic ski touring.

Go out and explore for yourself and see why the Radium area ranks among one of the top areas to backcountry ski in Western Canada. Enjoy.

Acknowledgements

From submitting photos to helping with details about the various trails and tours in the area, there are several local people who have helped with this book. Thanks to all of these people, without your help we would not have been able to complete this book on time.

We have personally skied most of the areas covered in this book. For the few that we haven't, we have relied on local input and information.

We would also like to extend a huge thank you to Hans Fuhrer for his advice and support and for his photos that truly saved the day for us.

A special thanks to our friend (M.W.) for editing our work. Any mistakes you find are due to our stubbornness in not following his advice.

RADIUM HOT SPRINGS

The tiny town of Radium Hot Springs is quietly becoming a centre for back-country skiers, and for good reasons. Located in the East Kootenays of British Columbia, in the upper Columbia Valley, Radium is situated between two separate mountain ranges: The Rocky and the Purcell Mountains. Both of these mountain ranges are quite different and unique.

The Rocky Mountains are a relatively young mountain range and boast dramatic, steep mountains with spectacular views. Although the weather is more severe and the snowpack shallower, the Rockies offer some areas with outstanding skiing.

The Purcell Mountains are a much older mountain range and typically offer terrain that is user friendly with an outstanding snowpack, and a milder climate. Because much of the Purcells have had mining and logging roads built through them in the past, this allows you to access these remote mountains with ease. The Purcells seem as if they were created with skiing in mind, offering expansive glaciers, outstanding scenery and world class skiing.

The town of Radium has a year round population of 600 and has a reputation as a summer destination. This leaves the town with an empty feeling in the winter. This means less crowds and cheaper room rates for the skiers visiting this area.

Radium offers several types of accommodations, from hostels and family run motels to upper scale resorts. This diversity and its low cost accommodations make for a comfortable place to base a ski holiday.

The town is named after its outdoor, natural and odourless hot springs. (A beautiful place to end a days skiing). The hot springs are open from noon until 10 pm everyday. There is a cost of $5 per person.

There are numerous amenities available in town. Several gas stations, garages, restaurants and pubs, grocery stores and motels make a trip to this area easy to arrange. With the exception of outdoor and ski equipment, the town has almost everything you'll need once you arrive.

Radium is home to one of the largest herds of Rocky Mountain Bighorn Sheep in North America. There are over 140 members in this herd, and when in comparison to the 600 people living here, they make up a large percent of the local population. The sheep are frequently seen wandering around town and definitely make up some of the charm this area has to offer.

We invite you to come and get away from the crowds that many nearby ski towns are struggling with. Enjoy our laid-back feeling and slow pace of life. Its what makes Radium what it is.

SKIING IN THE RADIUM AREA

This book is to be used as a reference. It is assumed, if you are heading into the backcountry, that you will have the appropriate skills, experience and equipment to deal with situations as they arise. We have not held your hand through the tours in this book, but rather have given you an idea of location, access and terrain. Compiling the details needed to safely complete the trips in this book is the responsibility of the reader.

Grades

Nordic skiing generally involves travel along trackset or groomed trails. Destinations are obvious and minimal hazards exist.

Light ski touring may involve trail breaking and crossing the bottom of avalanche run-out zones, but generally does not involve skiing in avalanche terrain. Mountain hazards such as open water, heavy snow, remoteness and navigation may exist.

Alpine ski touring is classified as skiing in, at or above treeline. Alpine terrain and destinations are usually the objective. Research of route and use of maps are necessary. Many hazards exist.

Destination slopes are areas where ski descents are the objective. This involves mountain travel to access these areas and snowmobiles are often the recommended form of access. Many hazards exist.

Hazards

Many hazards may be encountered in the backcountry. They are often unpredictable and frequently change with the elements. Hazards such as open water, extreme temperatures, deep or heavy snow, remoteness and difficult navigation may exist. If you are heading into avalanche terrain or going above treeline you may encounter avalanches, crevasses and serac falls, routefinding decisions, cliffs, whiteouts, long distance travel and exposure. Before attempting the tours in this book, you should have the skills and equipment to deal with the hazards you may encounter.

Maps

Topographical maps for the area can be obtained locally from the Government Agency office in Invermere. In Calgary contact Maptown at 403-215-4056 or if you can't access these locations contact:

Canada Map Office,
130 Bentley Avenue,
Nepean Ontario, KIA OE9,
phone 1-800-465-6277 or
613-952-7000.

All grid references given relate to maps issued from these locations. Maps in this book are not accurate and should not be relied upon. These maps are designed to give the reader an idea of the overview of an area.

Elevations

All elevations given are approximate and are given in metres. Gains and losses in altitude are expressed as vertical metres.

Distances and Directions

All distances given are approximate and are measured in Kilometres (km). Directions are given in the direction of travel. We have generally used major landmarks when giving directions.

Access

Weather can change the mode needed to access many of the areas in this book. What might be a 20 km ski one day might be a drive in an automobile the next. We often recommend a form of access; but this doesn't mean that other modes of travel are not useable or sometimes preferred.

Weather

Radium typically has a very mild climate by Canadian standards. Golf courses are often open till November and open in mid March. An average winter day in town is ⁻6° C. A cold snap usually occurs for one to four weeks every winter where temperatures can reach ⁻20° to ⁻30° C.

The weather in the mountains can be much more extreme. In winter an average day in the Rockies is ⁻10° to ⁻20° C and clear and sunny. An average day in the Purcells is ⁻5° to ⁻15° C and overcast. Although the weather around here is known to be friendly in comparison to surrounding areas, it is also unpredictable. Plan your trip accordingly.

Environment

Please help preserve our mountains by leaving no trace of your trip. Cutting or damaging of trees is prohibited in provincial and national parks.

Emergency Procedures

Self-reliance is a must in these mountains. Proper mountain skills and equipment should be acquired. For the more advanced trips in this book you should be prepared to deal with potential avalanches, inclement weather, glacier travel, whiteouts, route finding and first aid situations.

In case of emergency contact the Royal Canadian Mounted Police. They will be able to direct your call appropriately. Cell phones rarely work in the backcountry. Contacting local forestry companies or heli-ski operators with a radio is possible or carry a satellite phone as a form of safety insurance.

AVALANCHES

Avalanches are always a hazard when there is snow in the mountains. Every year people are involved in avalanches, and many prove fatal. The majority of these incidents happen during predictable snow conditions and on, or below, predictable slopes. Steps should be taken to ensure that this won't happen to you.

Several schools and institutes offer avalanche safety courses. Everybody that you travel with in the mountains should take an avalanche course to learn safe terrain choices, snowpack stability, routefinding skills and emergency procedures. We advise you re-take one of these courses every season. It easy to get a false sense of security as time passes. Read and review annually *Avalanche Safety for Skiers, Climbers and Snowboarders* by Tony Daffern, published by Rocky Mountain Books.

The skills needed are easy to achieve, but it can take years to acquire the experience needed to practically put them to use. At least one person in your party should have the experience needed to safely travel in avalanche terrain.

By watching the snowfall all year and recording the information, you can be very knowledgeable about an areas snowpack. If you don't live or frequent these mountains regularly there are several steps you can take before heading out. Call the Canadian Avalanche Association to get an idea about conditions for the area. Local ski resorts, outfitters and clubs may also be an excellent source of information. A little research will enable you to choose a trip appropriate to conditions you may encounter.

Everybody in your party should be equipped with an avalanche beacon, shovel and probe. Beacons should have compatible signals and fresh batteries. As technology increases, new products are becoming available to better deal with avalanches.

By being extremely cautious, and using all the skills and equipment available, you can safely enjoy the mountains for years to come.

The Toby Glacier. Photo: Chris Hofstetter.

EXPEDITIONS

Here are some areas that we have chosen to recommend for multi-day expeditions. The Toby Icefield is a beautiful and remote place. Although a little out of the geographical area covered in this book, the Hidden Towers also makes for a grand expedition. The Earl Grey Traverse provides a rewarding tour and a traverse from the Palliser River to the Mt. Assiniboine area and beyond offers limitless boundaries. For those of you who chose to do one of these tours, enjoy! You will be one of the few people to ever leave ski tracks in these magnificent areas.

We are assuming that you will extensively research any such area that you are planning to visit. Buy maps and study them. Find a route to access them and plan emergency exits. We recommend chartering a plane to get an aerial view of the area, in order to better understand the terrain. Local knowledge can be invaluable. You might want to consider food drops in strategic locations, in order to lighten the load on these long and demanding tours.

We urge you not to take these trips lightly. Be prepared, consider all of the "what ifs" that may be encountered and plan accordingly. Weather is a real factor in undertaking trips such as these. Spring generally has more stable weather than winter, but this is not to say that storms of epic proportions cannot last for weeks in the spring, leaving skiers stranded in precarious circumstances. Study the weather before heading out and leave your self extra days to sit out bad weather if need be. Certain areas are in wilderness reserves, and cannot be reached by air. This means that there will not be anyone to answer your call in an emergency. Being self-sufficient is a must. Know your limitations and plan accordingly.

EQUIPMENT

Nordic Skiing

The vast majority of nordic skiing in the Radium area occurs on groomed and trackset trails. Basic nordic skis, boots and bindings featuring either waxable or waxless bases are appropriate. When purchasing this type of equipment, focus on buying warm, comfortable boots. Warm, dry feet is perhaps the most important requisite for nordic skiing.

Light Touring

Many of the light ski tours described in this book will require the reader to break trails, cross creeks, negotiate moderate traverses and descend moderate slopes. Because of the more rugged nature of these tours, we strongly recommend the use of backcountry-style light touring or telemark skis. These skis have extra width for flotation in deep snow; yet possess a double-camber construction that affords excellent forward travel. Warm, waterproof and sturdy leather touring boots are highly recommended. Bindings should be of sufficient strength and quality to resist breakage. Cable bindings or Rotfella NNN Backcountry bindings are appropriate. Adjustable ski poles are recommended.

Alpine Ski Touring and Destination Slopes

The mountains surrounding Radium Hot Springs are remote and rugged. Alpine ski tours described in this book should not be attempted without serious backcountry equipment. Randonee (alpine touring) skis or modern shaped telemark skis are a must. Light telemark "skinny" skis would not be appropriate for most alpine tours in this book. Bindings should be of the highest quality possible—a broken binding could spell disaster in these mountains. Look for bindings that are light, easy to adjust and repair; and that have some form of heel lifter for climbing with skins. (The authors suggest the use of the excellent Alpine Trekker tm binding system for tours with advanced ski descents and for destination slopes. This system allows the skier to utilize the strength and DIN reliability of commercial downhill ski bindings when skiing aggressively.) Heel lifters reduce the strain on your Achilles' tendon when ascending considerable distances. Freeheel enthusiasts should wear plastic or double leather telemark boots.

Snowboarding

The destination slopes and several of the alpine tours in this book are ideal for snowboarders. With the exception of a small handful of destination slopes, you will need some means of ascending slopes. There are several products on the market that enable this, but we feel that a split design snowboard is the most practical. When used in combination with a set of climbing skins, a split board enables the snowboarder to travel anywhere a ski tourer would. Many of the available products are not practical for ascending slopes that require sidehilling and become a burden in deep, heavy snow. Adjustable ski poles are highly recommended.

SNOWMOBILES

In recent years, with the technological advancements of snowmobiles and the maintenance of groomed trails, snowmobiles have become an accepted form of access to the backcountry for many skiers.

People using randonee or snowboard setups will appreciate the ease of access snowmobiles offer. People attempting the alpine tours in this book will find a snowmobile will ensure more time is spent up in the mountains and less time travelling considerable distances from the valley bottoms.

We are not saying that you must use a snowmobile when we recommend it as a form of access. Helicopters and traditional ski access are also widely used in this area. We have recommended snowmobiles for economic and time saving reasons.

There are a few things to keep in mind when using snowmobiles in this area.

- Snowmobiles are not permitted in the local provincial and national parks or in the Purcell Wilderness Conservation area.

- A Land Use Act put into effect in 1999 by the provincial government restricts the use of snowmobiles in many areas. There are six alpine areas and numerous logging roads that are allocated for snowmobile use. Contact the local forestry office for more information.
- Snowmobiles can get you far out into the mountains, fast! This is great unless you break down or get stuck, leaving you tens or even hundreds of kilometres from civilization. Know how to do minor repairs and have the tools. Don't travel with only one snowmobile. Know how and have the equipment to free your machine from deep snow, steep hills and creeks or rivers.
- Expect the unexpected and always have the equipment, food and water to get home if your machine breaks down.
- As groomed snowmobile trails operate like a two way street, expect oncoming traffic.
- You are allowed to ski almost anywhere, but snowmobilers are only allowed on certain slopes. If these are the slopes you are skiing don't get annoyed if your favourite line gets tracked up. Most snowmobilers and skiers get along in this area quite well.
- For multiday trips, a toboggan pulled behind a snowmobile may enable you to bring the luxuries you might not normally have along.
- If you are using the groomed snowmobile trails in the area, it is mandatory that you purchase a trail pass from the Windermere Valley Snowmobile Society.
- Always wear a helmet and drive safely.

THE RADIUM AREA

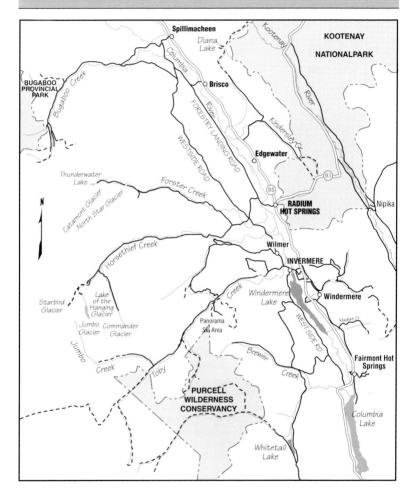

Opposite: Locals getting creative.
Photo: Ted Johnson.

Nordic Centres

BECKIE SCOTT NORDIC CENTRE
PANORAMA MOUNTAIN VILLAGE

nordic ski trails

The Beckie Scott Nordic Centre at Panorama Village is only a half-hour drive from Radium. With over 20 kilometres of groomed trails, featuring both classic and skate skiing, the Centre offers a mix of trails and outstanding scenery.

The trails have been in existence since 1992 and are improving yearly. Grooming occurs twice a week, on a variety of terrain. Trails on the golf course are suited for beginners while intermediate and advanced skiers will enjoy the trails following the south side of Toby Creek. A new warming hut, 6 km from the lodge, makes for a convenient location to have a break.

The Greywolf Lodge is open from 9 am to 5 pm, from mid December until late March. Snacks and refreshments are available as well as ski and snowshoe rentals. There is a charge of $15 per day, per person or you can buy a seasons pass for $60. Family and child discounts are available. If you are new to the sport or need to brush up on your skills, lessons are available. For more information call 250-342-6941 ext. 3840 or online at skipanorama.com.

Getting There

From Radium, travel south on Highway 93/95 for 12 km to the obvious traffic lights. Turn right and follow the signs to Panorama Mountain Village for a farther 20 km. Turn left across the bridge into the resort village and follow the main road to the nordic centre.

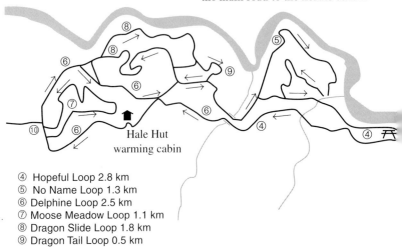

Hale Hut
warming cabin

④ Hopeful Loop 2.8 km
⑤ No Name Loop 1.3 km
⑥ Delphine Loop 2.5 km
⑦ Moose Meadow Loop 1.1 km
⑧ Dragon Slide Loop 1.8 km
⑨ Dragon Tail Loop 0.5 km
⑩ Barbour Creek Trail 8.4 km

Beckie Scott became the first North American woman to win an Olympic medal in cross-country skiing when she won a bronze medal for Canada in in the Pursuit race at the Salt Lake City OlympicWinter Games. During her nine years on the Canadian Cross Country Ski Team, through a rare combination of talent, hard work and determination, Beckie has re-written the Canadian record book and firmly established herself as one of the world's best cross-country racers. An ardent advocate of drug-free sport, in 2001 Beckie spearheaded an athletes' petition demanding the establishment of an independent drug-testing body for all World Cup and Olympic competitions.

To quote Beckie, "When you take on a goal and put your heart and soul into doing everything it takes to accomplish that goal, that is excellence."

Photo: Arnd Hemmersbach.
Courtesy Cross Country Canada.

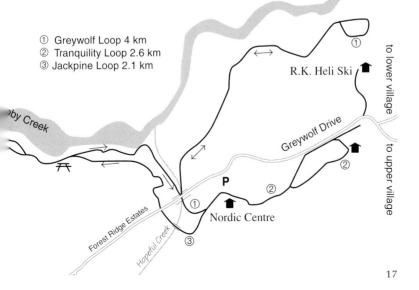

① Greywolf Loop 4 km
② Tranquility Loop 2.6 km
③ Jackpine Loop 2.1 km

BAPTISTE LAKE

nordic ski trails

Baptiste Lake offers a trackset trail system for nordic skiers. Groomed weekly and offering straightforward classic style trails, Baptiste makes for an enjoyable day of skiing close to town.

The trails are set on old logging roads and are centred around a small lake. Easy to follow and offering little hazards, these trails are ideal for newcomers to the sport or those looking for a relaxing day in a picturesque setting.

There is a charge of $3 per person per day to use the trails. A collection box is located at the trailhead. Depending on snow conditions, this network of trails is typically useable from late December until early March.

Getting There

From the 4-way stop in Radium, travel north on Highway 95. After 9.6 km, turn right on Hewitt Road. Follow Hewitt Road for 1.2 km to the plowed parking area on your right. The trail system begins on the other side of the open gate.

NIPIKA TOURING CENTRE nordic ski trails

The Nipika Touring Centre is on its way to becoming the largest nordic ski area of its kind in Western Canada. Noted for its remote atmosphere, great skiing and outstanding scenery, Nipika is a must do for all nordic skiers. Combined with its accommodations and facilities, this location is one of the premier areas covered in this book.

Using modern Bachler and Jaca grooming equipment, Nipika grooms over 40 kilometres of trails and has plans for expansion. Trails are groomed for both classic and skate skiing. A scenic 7 km trail is groomed for those of you who bring your dogs along. The trails are designed using a loop system

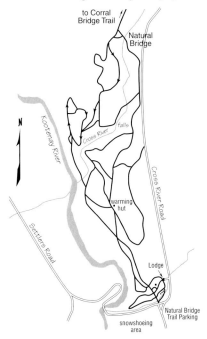

and offer a variety of terrain. Trails from the lodge to the Cross River are rated as beginner/intermediate, while trails across the Natural Bridge are rated intermediate/advanced.

Two charming warm up/lunch huts are ideally situated at trail junctions and offer convenient places to rest your legs. The Yearling Hut was built in 1920; using hand hewn logs and is located on the edge of a meadow with rising peaks to gaze at in the distance. The other hut is located 2 km from the lodge and makes an excellent destination for the kids.

The true charm of this area is its remote feeling. Located in the Kootenay River Valley, and bordering Kootenay National Park, Nipika gets you away from it all while only a short half-hour drive from Radium.

Nipika offers fantastic accommodations and facilities. A typical season starts in late November and lasts until the end of March. There is a cost of $5 per person per day to use the trail system. For more information phone 250-342-6516 or online at nipika.com.

Getting There

From Radium, drive east on Highway 93 into Kootenay National Park. After about 10 minutes turn right on Settlers Road (well marked). Drive this road for 13 km, following signs to Nipika Touring Centre. Be careful, as this road sees a lot of commercial traffic. Park in the day use lot, where there is a collection box for trail fees.

Purcells Tours & Destination Slopes

THE BUGABOOS

The Nunataks, the Spillimacheen Spires, or the Bugaboos: The names will change, but one thing remains constant. The "Bugs" are the home to massive glaciers, granite spires and amazing skiing. The views alone make this region one of the premier areas covered in this book.

The Bugaboo Creek drainage was first explored in 1906 by a group of miners and a small mining boom soon followed. In 1910 a party of mountaineers and explorers made their way up Bugaboo Creek in search of the famous Spillimacheen Spires. What they found was beyond their imagination, and thus followed a century of mountaineering and skiing.

In 1958 a party of skiers used the Bugaboos as a starting point for a traverse to the famed Rogers Pass. Since that day, numerous parties have followed this traverse and are now using the area as a touring destination.

1964 marked the beginning of a new era for the Bugaboos. A group of visionaries realized the potential of this area for skiing. Instead of installing traditional ski lifts, they dreamed of using a helicopter as a means of getting skiers to the top of the mountains. This was the birthplace of the industry now known as heli-skiing.

Whether you visit this area for a day of outstanding descents, or for an extended exploration trip, you will not be disappointed. The quantity and quality of snow, the awe-inspiring views, and the incredible skiing, make the "Bugs" a truly special place.

Photo: Ted Johnson

Getting There

From Radium, travel north on Highway 93 to the town of Brisco. Turn left at the sign to the Bugaboo Provincial Park. Cross the Columbia Valley on this road and follow the signs to the CMH Heli-ski lodge. Depending on logging activity this road will be plowed to various distances each year. Park well out of the way of logging traffic. All of the areas covered in the "Bugs" are accessed from this road.

BUGABOO PARK
Alpine touring

Bugaboo Park offers some of the best ski touring in North America. The views are "out of this world," with massive glaciers and huge granite spires. The skiing varies from glacier touring to ski mountaineering with steep descents.

The Conrad Kain Hut makes a great base for multi-day trips. A one day trip would not serve this area justice. The approach up the Bugaboo Glacier demands mountaineering and glacier skills and should not be taken lightly. If you have the skills and experience needed to reach this area the rewards will be well worth the effort.

Because of the nature of the wide open alpine terrain, a trip to the Bugaboos should be saved for periods of sunny, stable weather. There is no tree skiing in the event of overcast weather,

and retreating down the Bugaboo Glacier might not be possible if the visibility is bad. The terrain in the Bugaboos can best be described as huge. Huge glaciers and huge slopes are all part of the allure, but add substantially to the hazards. The Kain Hut itself lies in the path of a substantial avalanche path. The hut has been hit in the past. This is no place for skiers that are unsure of their mountain skills and experience.

Access
Skins, Sleds or Helicopter
From where you park your car, continue up the road, following the CMH signs by snowmobile. Once at the lodge you have two choices: One is to leave your snowmobile here and start skinning up Bugaboo Creek to the Bugaboo Glacier. Most

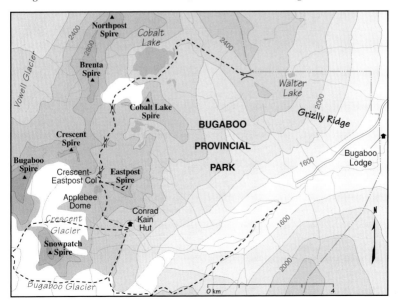

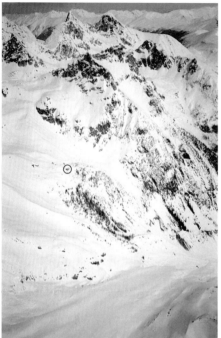

Looking down the Bugaboo Glacier from the shoulder of Snowpatch Spire. Kain Hut circled.

Photo: Ted Johnson

Skiing

The Bugaboos offer fantastic alpine touring on wide open terrain. Many tours include skiing in avalanche terrain. We have chosen some of the more obvious and popular ski routes, but the choices and possibilities in this area are endless.

The Vowell Glacier offers amazing touring with great views of Pigeon Spire, Bugaboo Spire, and the Howser Spires. There are two options to gain the Vowell Glacier from the Kain Hut. One is to ascend the Bugaboo/Snowpatch Col and the other is to wrap around the southeast side of Snowpatch Spire. This route crosses the top corner of the Bugaboo Glacier before gaining the Vowell glacier.

There are several excellent runs leading back to the Kain Hut. The Bugaboo/Snowpatch Col and the Eastpost/Crescent Col are two of the more obvious runs.

The northeast slopes of Eastpost Spire offer a great run down to an unnamed lake. To access these runs traverse through the Eastpost/Crescent Col and then ascend the wide open slopes on the northeast side of Eastpost Spire.

Another popular tour is to travel to Cobalt Lake. There is also an option of gaining Grizzly Ridge on the east side of Cobalt Lake and descending through treed slopes down a summer hiking trail back to the heli-ski lodge. This option makes for an interesting traverse of the Bugaboo area.

parties ascend the left (south) side of the glacier and slowly traverse to the right side, where the glacier levels out slightly. At this point ascend up the right side until you gain a bench under Snowpatch Spire. Traverse this bench towards the Kain Hut.

Another option is to fly into the Kain Hut from the CMH lodge with Alpine Helicopters. Arrangements must be made in advance. Although this option saves you from having to ascend the Bugaboo Glacier, the skills required to ski safely in this area are still required. The glaciers are most likely going to be your primary skiing objective and descent route home.

SILVER BASIN

Alpine touring

Silver Basin is a good alternative to Bugaboo Park. The approach is much less demanding, the skiing is fun and the views are spectacular. For parties who want to do a day trip to the Bugaboos, without any glacier travel, Silver Basin is the answer. Although somewhat spoiled by the amount of heli skiing, this still makes for a great spot to spend a day.

Access

From where you park your car, snowmobile up the Bugaboo Forest Service Road, following the signs to the heli ski lodge. Continue past the lodge and cross the bridge over Bugaboo Creek. 100 m past the bridge there is a sign on your right to Silver Basin. Park your snowmobile here. Ski up the road for 1.2 km until you reach a creek drainage. From here ascend for another 1 km until you reach a wide-open bowl. In total, you will gain approximately 250 vertical metres.

Skiing

Skiing in the Silver Basin area ranges from open alpine runs to perfectly gladed tree skiing.

The basin itself offers great skiing. By gaining the high ridge at the back of the basin you will be treated to outstanding views of Bugaboo Glacier and the spires that have made this area famous.

You will probably have noticed many heli-ski runs cutting through the trees on your way up to the basin. These

Silver Basin from above Bugaboo Creek.
Photo, Ted Johnson.

Silver Basin and Mount Frenchman. Photo: Ted Johnson

runs, as well as following the basin down, all lead to the road you left your snowmobile on. By skiing back up the road towards the lodge, you will return to your starting point.

When skiing up the east side of the basin, it is fairly straightforward to reach the top of Frenchman Mountain. From there you can ski down any of the obvious heli-ski runs back towards the lodge and your snowmobile. Use caution, as slopes off the north side of the ridge can be extremely steep.

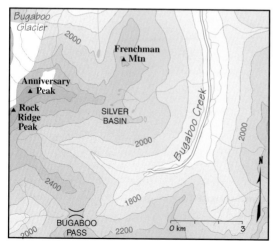

ROCKY POINT

Rocky Point is "the place" to go skiing with a snowmobile in this book. Although getting there presents its own problems and hazards, once there the area has several slopes which have snowmobile access and shuttle capabilities.

Rocky Point is big, remote country and should not be taken lightly. Until dedicated, local sledders break trail into the basin—usually in February or March—Rocky Point would be inaccessible by snowmobile. Some parties visit the area earlier in the year and skin up the valley to reach the bowls at the end of the valley. The snowmobile trail crosses several large avalanche paths and appropriate precautions should be taken.

A spring day in Rocky Point, with blue skies and good snow, will enable parties to get in a lot of vertical with minimal effort on huge wide open slopes.

Access

Snowmobile up the Bugaboo Forest Service Road until you reach a sign on the right hand side labelled "Rocky Point Recreation Area". On a typical year you will have to snowmobile for approximately 18 km. At this point the snowmobile trail becomes a single track trail and steeply swithchbacks five times before following the east side of Rocky Point Creek. Several large avalanche paths are crossed as the trail winds its way through the forest. If you are here after a large snowfall, and the trail has filled in, it would be easy to lose your way. If there

Skiers descending off the west ridge of Rocky Point. The repeater tower is just out of view to the left. Photo: Richard Paradis.

are no obvious snowmobile tracks once you leave the Bugaboo Forest Service Road at the sign to Rocky Point, you might want to reconsider coming here.

Skiing

This area offers fantastic snowmobile shuttle skiing. Combined with a bit of hiking, Rocky point offers world class skiing on a variety of terrain. From long cruiser runs to steep technical lines, this area has it all. The area is big mountain terrain and should not be taken lightly, as many of the slopes are prone to large avalanches. The area is very popular with the snowmobile crowd on the weekends and in the spring.

There is an obvious bowl straight ahead of you as you

Looking uo toward the northwest bowl. Photo: Ted Johnson.

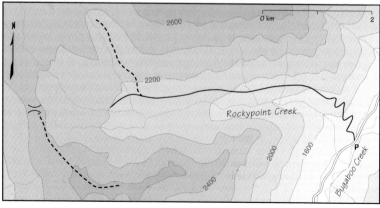

Ted Johnson preparing to board down the northwest bowl. Photo: Chris Hofstetter.

break out of treeline. Several ski possibilities exist in this area. Much of the terrain can be snowmobile shuttled, and in combination with some short hikes offers alpine runs of up to 2000 vertical feet.

There is another less obvious bowl to the northwest. After you snowmobile out of treeline turn to your left (west) and start descending toward the valley bottom, again always staying west, whenever possible. You should be able to see a radio antennae on the ridge to the west, with a drainage running up toward it. This drainage will lead into a wide open-bowl. It is possible in good conditions to snowmobile shuttle up to

the radio antennae. The slopes off of this ridge offer long and steep mountain terrain. The bowl at the top of the drainage offers more moderate slopes that can also be snowmobile shuttled. The slopes off of the west side of the radio antennae ridge are also popular ski slopes.

Given the right conditions and weather, Rocky Point can be a magical place. The views of the Bugaboo Spires to the west, the size of the alpine slopes and the quality and abundance of snow, combine to make this one of the premier destination slopes covered in this book.

FORSTER CREEK

Forster Creek lies directly west of Radium in the Purcell Mountains. Travel by plowed dirt roads lead to a groomed snowmobile trail that follows Forster Creek to its headwaters.

The water from Forster Creek is used by the town of Radium as its source drinking water. A new water treatment plant was built in the summer of 1999.

Forster Creek was named after Colonel Harold Forster, an alpinist, miner and rancher who settled in the area in the late 1890s. In 1898, Harold bought the Firlands Ranch and built a spacious home complete with tennis courts and a croquet lawn. After a night of drinking, Colonel Forster was shot dead by a young Indian friend and his house was burned to the ground.

Getting There:

From Radium, head west at the 4-way stop and follow the paved road through a residential part of town. Just before the mill turn left on the obvious gravel road (Horsethief Forest Service Road). Follow this road through the 4-way stop until you reach a road on your right (at the 13 km marker). Turn onto the Forster Forest Service Road. Shortly after you have crossed the bridge just past the water reservoir you will encounter a "Y" in the road, stay left. This is the groomed snowmobile trail that you will follow to the trailhead. Depending on logging activities, this road will be plowed to different locations each year.

Looking up toward Scotch Peaks and the approach to the Catamount Glacier. Photo: Chris Hofstetter.

The Irish Peaks loom over the Welsh Lakes. Photo: Ted Johnson

WELSH LAKES
Alpine touring

The Welsh Lakes area offers a beautiful tour up a seldom visited valley with a group of three lakes to explore, several slopes for skiing on and some of the finest mountain scenery in the area. A perfect location for a day of exploring big rolling alpine terrain.

Getting There

Snowmobile: Follow the groomed snowmobile trail to the 36 km marker. There will be a sign on your left indicating the Welsh Lakes.

Skiing

Begin by skiing up the well marked trail to the Welsh Lakes area. After 5.5 km and an elevation rise of 460 m, you will arrive at the first of three lakes. The

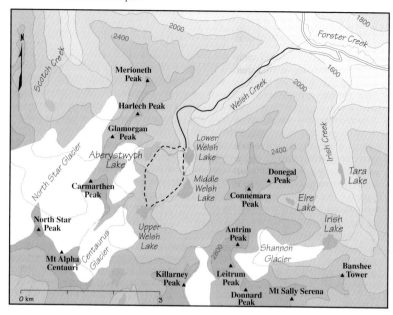

views are outstanding and only get better farther up this valley. The second lake is located behind and above the first, and the third is to the west and above the second lake. We recommend skiing in this area when you are sure of the snow conditions as you will be skiing up large, wide-open slopes in order to gain the upper two lakes.

There are several possibilities for slopes to ski on. The descent from the third lake back down to the first lake offers several route options, from easy to extreme.

For parties with intermediate mountain travel experience, gaining the first lake presents little problems and makes for an adventurous outing.

FORSTER BASIN

The Forster Basin provided some of the best alpine touring in the area. With two cabins in the basin and another within touring distance, Forster is definitely worth a multi-day visit. It receives an abundance of snow and has a typical season lasting from November till May. Much of the skiing is ideally suited for alpine touring, but we feel that the Forster Basin itself is worth its own section in the book due to its ease of access and the many possibilities for excellent ski descents. Although the area is popular with snowmobilers,

many of the ski slopes are in snowmobile restricted areas or are on slopes not suitable for snowmobiles.

Access

Snowmobile: Follow the groomed snowmobile for 26 km from the water treatment plant. This will deliver you to the edge of the basin and the Windermere Valley Snowmobile Societies Cabin.

Helicopter: Some parties use a helicopter to access this area. You can get dropped off at any of the three cabins .

Excellent terrain surrounds the headwall at the end of the basin. Photo: Ted Johnson.

The south side of Forster Basin offers excellent descents.

Ted en route to another fine tree run above the Dave Whyte Hut. Photo: Chris Hofstetter.

The north side of the basin offers some great tree skiing with possibilities of some long alpine runs. Unfortunately, some of the open areas on this aspect see a lot of snowmobile traffic.

There is an open alpine headwall at the end of the basin which leads to a set of lakes and eventually up to the Catamount glacier. The headwall offers some exciting terrain with runs averaging 200 vertical meters and if in condition can be snowmobile shuttled by experienced parties. This area can see a lot of snowmobile traffic.

These are some of the most obvious places to ski, but there are endless possibilities in this area.

Ted en route to the south side of the basin. Photo: Chris Hofstetter.

Skiing

This area offers excellent descents on a wide variety of terrain and aspects.

The slopes on the south side of the basin offer some open alpine slopes with a wide variety of terrain choices. Snowmobiles are not allowed on this side of the basin, which offer fantastic skiing on north facing slopes.

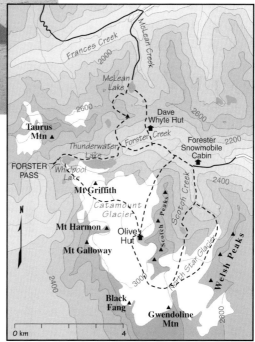

Mount Harmon, Catamount Glacier. Photo: Hans Fuhrer.

An aerial view of the ridge separating Forster Basin and Maclean Lake area. The Dave Whyte Hut is just below the bottom left of the photograph. Photo: Ted Johnson

UPPER FORSTER
Destination slopes

The Forster area offers perhaps the best alpine touring in this book. With three huts, several large glaciers, fun tree skiing, steep to gentle terrain and a season that can start in November and last to early June, Forster is an area that is popular for a reason.

Getting There
Snowmobile: Follow the groomed snowmobile trail 26 km from water reservoir. This trail will deliver you to the local snowmobile cabin. The trail is generally groomed once a week, but can get quite rough due to amount of traffic it sees.

Skiing
The upper Forster offers several possibilities for ski touring. The Forster Basin runs east to west and will be used as a reference when describing the tours in the area. This area receives an abundance of good quality snow, which can provide a long season. People are often skiing in this area in early November and it is not uncommon to be able to enjoy a spring tour right into June. The true attraction to the Forster area is its diversity in skiable terrain. Large ice caps, sweeping glaciers, steep slopes, tree skiing for cloudy days and gentle tours through large

meadows and lakes are some of the features offered in the area.

At the west end of the basin lies a headwall that leads to a set of lakes. During winter when the snow is deep, snowmobilers cannot gain this headwall. When the snow is consolidated, the lakes are overrun by snowmobiles and should probably be left alone. To gain the headwall, most parties will ascend the obvious creek bed on the north end of the headwall for 120 m before turning left (west) along the obvious bench that angles upwards towards Thunderwater Lake. This area offers many possibilities for skiing as well as many enjoyable lines back down to the basin. At the far end of this lake and slightly to the south, there is a pass that leads up to Whirlpool Lake. Another beautiful spot high in the alpine. The Whirlpool Glacier begins at the southwest end of the lake and leads up to the Catamount Glacier.

Tracks descending from Catamount Glacier toward Forster Basin. Photo: Chris Hofstetter.

The Catamount Glacier is a large expanse of ice that offers great touring and some enjoyable peaks to ascend. There is a cabin on the edge of the glacier that makes for a nice spot to spend a few days, because one day will not do this area justice. There are three commonly used routes to gain the glacier, and each offers its own rewards and challenges.

Gain the headwall at the east end of Forster Basin, and cross Thunderwater Lake, Whirlpool Lake and the Whirlpool Glacier to the east tip of the Catamount. This is a spectacular route up onto the glacier.

Another route onto the Catamount involves ascending the North Star Glacier. At the east end of Forster Basin there is a valley heading south. By making your way through the trees you will soon break out into the alpine and the toe of the North Star. Most parties stay left (east) and follow the curving glacier up to the Catamount. This route offers little route finding difficulties, although if its your first visit to the area you might have to poke around a bit in order to gain the Catamount at the top of the North Star Glacier. A straightforward pass is easily crossed between the two glaciers which seemingly blend into each other. Most parties use this as a descent route due to the fantastic run it offers.

The third and probably the easiest way to gain the Catamount is by ascending the slopes to the northeast of the Scotch Peaks. Half way down the Forster Basin, on its south side there is

an obvious draw that leads up to a bench, another slope that hugs the large rock outcropping on the left (west) leads up to the glacier. These slopes are almost directly across the basin from the Dave Whyte Hut.

The Catamount area is not a place to be if the weather craps out. It would be extremely easy to get disorientated and lose your way. Parties skiing in this area should be able to navigate in whiteout conditions. Although not heavily crevassed during winter, all three of the glaciers mentioned do require good glacier and route finding skills in order to travel them safely.

On the north side of the Forster Basin there is a long ridge that separates the basin from the next valley over. On the other side of this ridge lies Maclean Lake and some fun ski terrain. There are a couple of commonly used routes that lead to this area. Probably the

A view of the exceptional run down the North Star Glacier. Photo: Ted Johnson.

to North Star Glacier

to Forster Basin

Aerial view of the Catamount Glacier. Olive Hut circled. Photo: Scott Barnsby.

easier of the two is located at east end of the basin. At the north end of the headwall at the end of the basin, there is a creek bed that climbs to the north. By making your way up to the obvious pass at the top it is an easy ski down to the meadows on the far side. If you travel south through these meadows and following the obvious bench you will arrive at the Maclean Lake area. Another route to the Maclean area is to ascend the slopes directly above the Dave Whyte Hut. There are a couple of passes along this ridge that offer exciting skiing down the other side. Some of these routes will require hopping off cornices in order to gain the slopes on

the north side. The pass directly above and slightly to the east offers the easiest route. This area is the site of an avalanche fatality involving a young local skier; the cabin below was built in his memory.

There are endless possibilities for skiing in the Forster area, we have listed the most popular but many other tours exist. Have fun exploring this area, a lifetime of skiing is available.

This area is only somewhat tainted by the amount of snowmobile traffic during the spring, despite a closure to snowmobiles, they manage to track up nearly all of the glaciers and a large percentage of the skiable slopes.

HORSETHIEF CREEK

Southwest of Radium in the Purcell Mountains lies Horsethief Creek. The creeks drains several large glaciers and tumbles through spectacular canyons and waterfalls into the Columbia River.

Travel to Horsethief Creek from Radium is on the Horsethief Creek Forest Service Road, which is usually plowed for 17 kilometres. Plowing normally stops shortly after the turn off to Forster Creek. From here most parties use a snowmobile to access the fantastic skiing this drainage has to offer.

Local lore has it that this creek was named after a rogue who stole some horses from a group of whiskey peddlers in the 1880s. After making his escape up this valley he was swept to his death after trying to cross this swift flowing creek.

Getting There

From the 4-way stop in Radium travel south on Forsters Landing Street through a residential part of town. Turn left on the Horsethief Forest Service Road, just before the large wood mill. This road eventually follows the Horsethief Creek to the three trailheads in this section of the book. Depending on logging activity in the area it will be plowed to different locations each year. Snowmobiles are then used to gain access to the described tours.

Ted crossing Horsethief Creek.
Photo: Chris Hofstetter.

41

MCDONALD CREEK

The McDonald Creek drainage offers stunning views and an old mining town. An enjoyable place to visit that offers snowmobile access into the upper reaches of the basin. The skiing is somewhat limited but for parties looking for a day of uncomplicated touring along old roads, with mountains soaring up into the sky, McDonald is the place.

Getting There

Snowmobile up the Horsethief Creek Forest Service Road to the 36 km marker. Turn left up the marked road and follow it up into the basin at the end of the Mcdonald Valley.

Skiing

Most of the skiing in this area consists of scenic tours along old mining and logging roads. Snowmobiles use this area, although somewhat infrequently.

There is an old mining town, Redline Mine, scattered along the southeast end of the valley. A few of the old mining buildings have been maintained and offer a comfortable place to get out of the elements.

A good rule of thumb for this area would be that the higher you get the better the views. The old roads are too numerous to list, many gain substantial altitude along the east side of the valley and provide amazing views of the Farnham Tower. At 11,342 feet Farnham Tower is the highest mountain in the Purcells.

Options

The Redline Glacier, at the far end of the basin, can be skied and offers a couple of intricate descents.

Peter Pass, on the southwest end of the basin, can be travelled through to reach the Delphine Glacier. Most parties use McDonald as an exit, as the steep slope leading down into McDonald Creek is much easier to descend than to climb.

The approach onto the Redling Glacier can be seen at bottom left of the picture. Photo: Chris Hofstetter.

Morning sun peaks over the Farnham Glacier. Photo: Ted Johnson.

FARNHAM CREEK

Farnham Creek offers an easy to follow route up a valley with outstanding views of high peaks and tumbling glaciers. A great tour for skiers of all abilities. There are some outstanding options for skiers with advanced skills on large glaciers.

Getting There

Snowmobile up the Horsethief Forest Service Road to the 46 km marker. Park beside a well-built footbridge that crosses Horsethief Creek.

Skiing

Begin by skiing over the footbridge and following the old logging road that quickly gains altitude before levelling out into the Farnham Valley. After 2 km, a bridge crosses the creek and the route then follows an overgrown road on the other side, that follows Farnham Creek up the valley. Although somewhat overgrown and washed out in a few places, the route presents little difficulties. If you lose the route, stay close to the creek and you will pick it up again.

There is an old cabin 8.5 km along the tour, which makes a nice destination for most parties. The views of the Commander Glacier are breathtaking. A proposed ski resort threatens the future of this pristine area.

Options

For parties who want to explore the nearby glaciers, we recommend bringing winter camping gear and spending a few days in the area. It would be an extremely long day to ski the glaciers and exit in one day.

The Commander Glacier offers outstanding skiing. Crevasses and seracs are many and precise routefinding skills are a must. Runs of up to 1000 m are possible.

By following the left fork of Farnham Creek it is possible to ski on the Farnham Glacier. Great runs are plentiful in this area. A local heli ski operator has built a large cabin on the glacier and uses it extensively for skiing. This has definitely spoiled this remote place.

Chris skiing up Farnham Creek with the Commander Glacier in the background.
Photo: Ted Johnson.

An aerial view of the Lake of the Hanging Glacier. Photo: Ted Johnson.

LAKE OF THE HANGING GLACIER   Alpine touring

Lake of the Hanging Glacier is just what it implies. A large frozen lake with glaciers surrounding it and pouring directly into it. The scenery is the basis of this tour, which gains 700 m over 8 km and requires travel across and up large open slopes. A truly unique and beautiful destination.

Getting There

Snowmobile up the Horsethief Forest Service Road to just past the 49 km marker. This is literally the end of the road. The tour begins behind the summer registry and outhouse.

Skiing

A mix of skiing through trees, across avalanche run-out zones and up large slopes make this tour best left for when you are sure of the snow stability.

Although the route up is fairly straightforward, route finding skills are a must. Follow Farnham Creek on its right side for 3 km to a metal bridge that crosses the creek. Cross this bridge and continue following the Horsethief Creek for a further 1.5 km to where a creek that descends from the lake joins Horsethief Creek. Switchback your way up the large slopes following this tributary creek until the terrain levels out and leads to your destination.

Views of the Jumbo Glacier at the far end of the lake, the Lieutenant Peaks and Glacier Dome form a backdrop that will etch itself into your mind for years to come. Truly a special place.

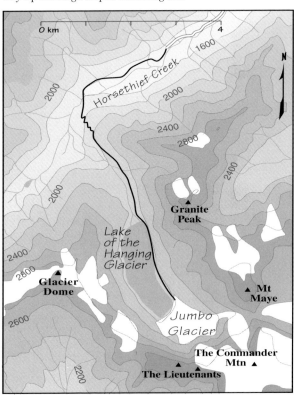

TOBY CREEK

The Toby Creek drainage offers a wide variety of skiing: From easy light tours; fantastic destination slopes and some high quality alpine ski touring and traverses. This drainage has it all.

The Toby Creek drainage has been inhabited for over 130 years. There has been mining in this area for many years and the roads built by the mining companies provide easy access to some great ski areas.

The creek was named after Dr. Toby, from Colville Washington, a prospector who settled in the area in 1964. He was successful in finding several sites that were home to a number of prosperous mines.

Getting There

From Radium, travel south on highway 93/95 for 12 km to the obvious lights. Turn right and follow the signs to panorama Mountain Village. All of the tours and areas found in the Toby Creek section are described from here.

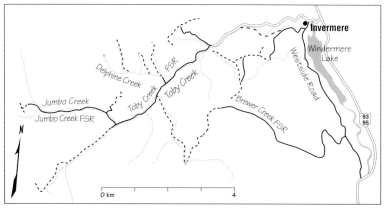

PARADISE BOWL Destination slopes

Paradise Bowl is popular for good reason. Easy travel on paved roads and a short snowmobile ride bring you to this outstanding alpine bowl. Fantastic views, great alpine descents and snowmobile shuttle tree runs are some of the features that make this area so exceptional. Although somewhat overrun by commercial and private snowmobilers, many fine ski descents are possible in the area.

Getting There

A plowed parking area on the left side of Toby Creek Road serves a launching point for parties travelling up to Paradise Bowl. Located 2 km before Panorama Mountain Resort.

Access

Snowmobile: From the parking area, cross the road and field to the obvious groomed snowmobile trail, follow the well marked trail for 12.5 km to an old mine site in the bottom of the bowl, a further 1 km will bring you to the cabin

Note

Please respect the rights of Toby Creek Adventures. They lease the land you will be crossing and they maintain the trail and cabin. Please give all tours the right of way. Toby Creek Adventures rents avalanche equipment and offers skier shuttles to the bowl. You can contact them by calling 250-342-5047.

Skiing

One of the true highlights of the Paradise area is the excellent tree skiing available on overcast days. A local heli-ski company has cut many excellent fall line

Photo: Ted Johnson.

runs that cross the groomed snowmobile trail on the way to the bowl. This makes snowmobile shuttles a quick and easy way to gets lots of vertical in a day. Runs average 150–900 m.

The ridge above the cabin on the north side of the bowl offers fantastic views and wide open alpine runs. To gain the ridge, leave your snowmobile at the cabin and skin back down the groomed trail for about 100 metres and turn left on the less travelled road. Follow this road to where it reaches the tree line. Most parties gain the ridge by skinning up from here. Once on the ridge there are a few different possibilities. By turning east on the ridge, the south facing slopes offer an excellent run in combination with the earlier described tree runs, If you turn west on the ridge you can reach many outstanding descents back into the bowl on south facing slopes.

Chris enjoying another shuttle run, Paradise Bowl. Photo: Ted Johnson.

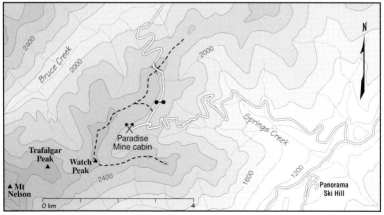

DELPHINE CREEK & DELPHINE GLADES   Destination slopes

A straightforward ski tour up a logging road with outstanding views. Easy access, reliable snow and an easy to follow trail, make this trip popular.

In good snow years, the Delphine Glades offer some excellent open and steep tree runs. Due to the ease of access and the terrain, this area can make for a great day of skiing when visibility is poor.

Getting There

Instead of turning right across the bridge into Panorama Mountain Village, continue following Toby Creek Road for a farther 8.2 km to a small plowed area on the right side of the road.

Skiing

Skiing up the Delphine Road is relatively straightforward and a trail will often be broken. Immediately after leaving your car, the trail climbs a small hill. The rest of the trail is much gentler as it gradually climbs up the Delphine Valley. The first couple of kilometres give great views of a canyon. The trail then breaks out of the trees and you will be rewarded with tremendous views of towering alpine peaks. The trail will reach the head of the valley after 10 km, where you will be treated to spectacular views of several tumbling glaciers. Return on the same trail.

Skiing the Glades

Most of the glade skiing is done on the obvious slopes on your right (west facing) after travelling 3 km up the Delphine Road. There is an overgrown road, that bisects the two draws, offering some fun tree skiing. Most parties ascend through the trees approximately 300 m after the first switchback to gain the obvious glades above. By following the road for a farther 1 km you can turn right and head back up another unplowed road. This road branches and gives access to some steep tree skiing between the switchbacks.

Options

It is possible for those with mountaineering skills, and alpine touring equipment to gain the Delphine Glacier at the end of the valley. During the early 1980s, the Canadian Cross Country Ski Team used this glacier for training. It is then possible to travel through Peter Pass and into McDonald Creek.

It is also possible to ascend to the northwest end of the valley to Shamrock Lake and farther up to Black Diamond Col, where several skiing possibilities exist. The Farnham Glacier, or runs down the Black Diamond basin both offer demanding alpine tours.

Chris skiing in the Delphine Glades.
Photo: Ted Johnson.

THUNDERBIRD MINE

An easy ski tour up a well graded mining trail that leads to an old mining townsite. Three large avalanche paths must be crossed, so we recommend saving this one for a day when you are sure of the snow stability. There is limited skiing in the area but the views and an old cabin make this a nice overnight trip.

Getting There

Drive for 8.2 km past Panorama Mountain Resort to a small plowed parking area on the right. The tour begins by skiing up the unplowed road.

Skiing

The skiing in this area is partially described in the Delphine Glades. The skiing around the mining townsite is somewhat limited and exposed to avalanches. Most people ski this tour because of the old mining site and its accommodation, the spectacular views and the remoteness it offers.

Begin by skiing up the Delphine Creek Forest Service Road for 3 km until you see an overgrown road heading up into the trees. This road is located just before the first avalanche path crossing the Delphine Forest Service Road. The road will take left-hand switchback after about 100 m. Follow the road until you see another road

branching off to your right, follow this road for 2 more switchbacks where you will continue straight through instead of turning with the road. A good landmark is a large fallen down tree crossing this trail. After 6 km along this trail you will begin to traverse into the Sultana Creek drainage. From this point you start gradually climbing and cross 3 major avalanche paths. Use caution. The old townsite is located after the third path in a stand of trees. There is an elevation gain of 240 m between where you start traversing into the first avalanche path and where the town site is located. There is a cabin in the old town site that local skiers and hikers have maintained. If you use this cabin please be courteous and make sure you leave it sealed up and in a clean condition.

Kicking back after reaching the Thunderbird Cabin. Photo: Ted Johnson.

UPPER TOBY CREEK

An enjoyable ski tour in a remote valley which offers impressive scenery, an historic, rundown cabin and a great sense of remoteness.

Getting There

Drive up Toby Creek Road for 20 km past Panorama Mountain Village to the obvious plowed parking area. The road is not plowed past here.

Toby Icefield. Photo: Chris Hofstetter.

Skiing

There is a trail at the far (east) end of the parking area heading into the trees. This trail is a summer horse trail and might not be obvious during the winter if you arrive after a fresh snowfall or if it hasn't been travelled in a while. If you can't locate the trail, simply begin skiing up the valley staying on the north side of Toby Creek.

After approximately 3 km you will enter the runout of a large avalanche path. There is an old cabin on the southeast side of the opening about 150 m above the creek. This cabin was built for Governor Earl Grey in 1909 as a vacation spot for his family. Groups only wanting a short day will be satisfied with this area as the view of the Pharaoh Peaks and the pristine valley laid out in front of you is fantastic. Most parties will take a little under an hour to reach this point.

For parties that want a longer day, you can follow Toby Creek for a distance of 20 km from the parking area The views keep getting better the farther you ski, featuring a large glacier near the headwaters of the creek.

JUMBO CREEK

Jumbo Creek is a tributary of Toby Creek, and every spring drains the huge snowpack that makes Jumbo such a great place to ski. The skiing in this area is outstanding! A roomy cabin provides a comfortable place to spend a few days in the area. There are several possibilities for day trips, as well as a glacier that offers an enjoyable multi-day trip. Great snow and terrain make the Jumbo Valley extremely popular.

The Jumbo Valley is the object of a number of commercial plans. It is currently used extensively by a local heli ski operation, and is proposed as a site for a year round destination resort. The future of this area is uncertain at this time. The area is also a prime candidate for a provincial park. Restricting commercial business in Jumbo would guarantee its wilderness for years to come.

Above: The Jumbo area offers an abundance of snow. Photo: Ted Johnson.

Access

Most people ski up the Jumbo Creek Forest Service Road for approximately 11 km to where the tours in this book begin.

Start by skiing up the road to the right of the parking lot for 1.5 km. Stay left at a Y intersection. Almost immediately you cross over Jumbo Creek on a well made bridge. Turn right and follow this road (Jumbo Creek Forest Service Road) for 9 km to the next bridge. The trail between these two bridges crosses under multiple avalanche paths. Use caution. See map on page 46.

Many parties use snowmobiles to access the area. Although snowmobiles are prohibited in the Jumbo Valley, they are allowed along the route described but no farther. They can certainly speed up a trip, making many areas in Jumbo feasible to ski as a day trip. Sometimes the trail in, or on your way out, is buried under avalanche debris. Digging an L–shaped cut across the debris is often enough to get a snowmobile across.

Skiers on the ridge above Jumbo Pass Cabin. Photo: Richard Paradis.

JUMBO PASS

Alpine touring

One of the more popular areas covered in this book, and for good reason, Jumbo Pass offers a deep snowpack that starts early in the year. Early season skiing is often "doable" by late October or early November. A wonderful cabin situated on a rolling ridge makes an ideal base for a multi-day ski trip. Combine this with the outstanding ski terrain and you have a real gem. The diversity in skiable terrain makes this an area all types of backcountry skiers can enjoy.

Powder turns at Jumbo Pass.
Photo: Richard Paradis.

Getting There

From the bridge 9 km along the Jumbo Creek Forest Service Road, continue skiing up the road to a Y-junction (1 km). Stay left and continue for a short distance to an open area. From here there are a number of gullies and treed ridges you can follow to gain the pass. It is best to start switch-backing up through the trees from the opening, staying slightly right where possible. Once you gain the ridge stay right and follow the open, rolling ridge until you locate the cabin, which is situated at the far end of the ridge just before the

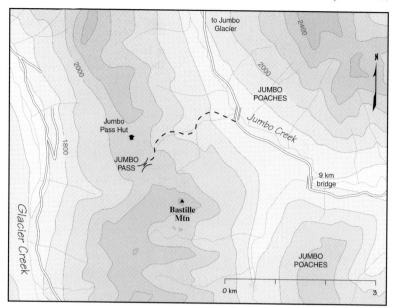

ridge dramatically steepens. A map and a GPS receiver may be useful if the weather is bad or you are arriving in the dark. I personally know of a few different parties that have spent the night in the trees after unsuccessfully trying to locate the cabin. The route is straightforward but can become confusing in a blizzard.

Skiing

The skiing off the pass and the extending ridges offers a nice mix of terrain. Tree skiing, big bowls and tight chutes are all here.

Tree skiing on the west side of the pass is gentle, open and a fun location for novices or on days when the weather or snowpack is less than ideal. Runs of 200 m are abundant all along the ridge.

The slopes on the east side of the pass and ridge offer some fantastic runs down to the Jumbo Creek Forest Service Road. Interesting creek formations make for some excellent lines. Tree runs are available between the open creeks and many have fun rolls and drops along the way. Runs of up to 600 m are abundant.

By gaining the ridge above the cabin you can access some great alpine terrain. The face back down to the cabin is short but sweet. Bowls and chutes off the northeast side of the ridge offer multiple steep runs, combine these with a ski to valley bottom for an unforgettable run of over 700 m.

These are some of the more popular areas to ski around the pass; there are also many other possibilities in the area. Enjoy!

Skiing down to Blockhead Col at head of Leo Creek between Jumbo Pass and Jumbo Poaches.
Photo: Hans Fuhrer.

JUMBO GLACIER

Alpine touring

The tour up to the Jumbo Glacier can either be done as a mellow trip up the gentle valley or as a more advanced trip for those who want to gain the glacier and ski to its rounded dome. Either way we recommend bringing a large pack as this tour is best done as a multi-day trip. An abundance of snow and outstanding scenery make a tour up this valley well worth the visit.

Skiing

For those folks planning a long easy tour, the skiing is straightforward. From the bridge at 9 km continue along the Jumbo Creek Forest Service Road, then the creekbed, until you find a safe location near the end of the valley to view the outstanding scenery. They're a few obvious locations near treeline that offer great views and a safe place to set up camp. Approximately 6 km from bridge to treeline.

Parties wishing to ascend the glacier should allow a full day for an ascent and descent. Skiing from your car along the road and up the glacier would be a very long day. There is a

The backside of Glacier Dome. Photo: Ted Johnson.

Looking down on Jumbo Glacier.
Photo: Ted Johnson.

steep headwall that must be climbed
to gain the glacier. Depending on snow
conditions you might have to kick
steps up it. From the top of the headwall there is an obvious route up the
glacier. Stay left nearing the top to
avoid the steepest section of the final
headwall then follow the rounded
ridge to the top. There is generally
sufficient snow to cover most of the
crevasses, but always use caution.
Views into the Farnham Creek, Lake of
the Hanging Glacier and the Stockdale
Glacier are amazing. The run down
your ascent route is a classic, enjoy!

JUMBO POACHES

Although the Jumbo Valley is best known for its cabin and the skiing that surrounds it, there are also several other slopes in the area that provide prime ski terrain. They are so good that a local heli-ski company uses them extensively and has even cut and thinned out the trees. These runs are mostly through open trees and are easy to get to and make a nice alternative to the popular pass.

Skiing

As you ski along the Jumbo Creek Forest Service Road beyond the bridge, there are several runs on the right side of the valley that offer excellent skiing. 2 km, 3 km and 4 km along this road are logical places to start an ascent. Runs of 500 m are typical. There are a few routes up into the alpine above the trees, which can add to a run in this area. Most of these runs are directly across the valley from Jumbo Pass.

Note

We have labelled these runs as destination slopes. This assumes you have used a snowmobile to travel on the Jumbo Creek Forest Service Road. It is not uncommon for many of these runs to have ski tracks on them from commercial heli-skiers.

BREWER CREEK

Brewer Creek is situated to the west of the town of Fairmont Hot Springs, 35 km south of Radium, in the Purcell Mountains.

This creek was named after Mr. and Mrs. Brewer who built the original Fairmont Hotel in 1888. Brewer Creek leads to some high alpine terrain ideally sculpted for ski touring. Most parties either ski or snowmobile up this road—from where winter plowing stops—to gain the high alpine terrain at the Brewer Creek headwaters.

Getting There

From Radium travel south on Highway 93/95 past the town of Fairmont Hot Springs. 2 km past Fairmont and just before the Hoodoo Resort, turn right onto Westside Road. 5 minutes along this road you turn left onto Hawke Road. Follow to the plowed parking lot or snowline. This road is usually plowed for snowmobilers as far as the parking area.

High alpine terrain in the Brewer Bowls. Photo: Pablo Fernandéz.

Darren Livingston telemarking at the Coffee Pot. Photo: Chris Hofstetter.

COFFEE POT

Destination slopes

The Coffee Pot is a collection of clearcuts that offer sweeping valley views, gentle snowmobile shuttle slopes and few natural hazards. A great spot for newcomers to the sport to make some safe and easy turns.

Getting There

Snowmobile. At the far end of the snowmobile parking lot in Brewer Creek there is an obvious groomed snowmobile trail. Eighty metres up this trail there is a sign "Coffee Pot" and a well beaten trail to the left. Follow this trail across a bridge and up several switchbacks before gaining the clearcuts.

Skiing

There are several wide open clearcuts in the area. Although not steep, many offer runs of up to 200 m, and almost all of these slopes can be shuttled with snowmobiles. There is little hazard from avalanches, due to the low angle of the terrain. A great location for inexperienced parties or those wanting an easy day with fantastic valley views. On a clear day, Mt. Assiniboine is visible far off in the Rockies.

BREWER BOWLS Expedition area

The Brewer Bowls are a collection of high alpine bowls, ridges and peaks that offer serious ski touring. Big mountains and big terrain make the Brewer area perfect for a multi-day trip.

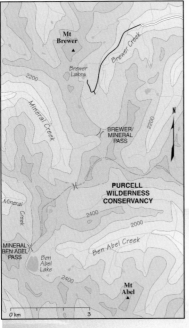

Getting There

Snowmobile: From the parking lot, snowmobile up the obvious groomed trail. Turn left on the second trail, which follows Brewer Creek for 13 km. You will arrive at a narrow footbridge. Grooming typically stops here but you can continue snowmobiling the final 5 km to the upper lakes. If you are breaking trail past this point it can get a little confusing, as the trail crosses a few meadows and climbs up the creek bed through narrow trees in two spots. These hills are quite steep and demand a modern snowmobile with traction and power. Many parties end up skinning the final few kilometres to the end of the creek.

Skiers on the ridge above Hopeful Bowls. Note the excellent skiing available. Photo: Scott Barnsby.

Slopes above the upper lake. Photo: Ted Johnson.

Helicopter: If you plan on spending a few days in the area you might want to consider using a helicopter for access. A good place to get dropped off at is on the upper lakes under Mt. Brewer. There are a few options for skiing out or you can get picked up by a pre-arranged helicopter.

Skiing

Although there is no cabin we recommend spending a few days in the area. Good weather and quality winter camping gear are needed here as there are many areas to ski. This area is a prime destination for exploring so we won't go into to much detail.

The slopes below Mt. Brewer and surrounding the lakes offer several possibilities for making turns as well as an enjoyable ridge to tour on.

An exciting option is to ski over to Mineral Creek and then into Ben Abel Creek. At this point you have entered the Purcell Wilderness Conservancy where there are lakes, valleys and ridges galore for your enjoyment.

A possible exit route is to ski over 3 ridges and drainages to gain a pass on the west side of Mt. Goldie. From here you can follow Hopeful Creek down into Panorama Mountain Village. This tour offers interesting route finding challenges as well as excellent skiing.

Touring through open alpine terrain, skiing on large slopes and following or crossing wind scoured ridges is the name of the game in the Brewer area. We highly recommend bringing a map, GPS receiver and compass, as it is easy to get lost here when the weather craps out. This area has seen avalanche fatalities in the past and should not be taken lightly.

Rockies Tours & Destination Slopes

MADIAS CREEK

A short ski tour that leads to a basin surrounded by dramatic mountain faces. When snow conditions permit, this tour makes for a nice, easy day. Hazards are limited and the views are outstanding.

Getting There

From Radium travel South on Highway 93/95 for 12 km to the obvious lights. Continue straight through the lights for another 13 km and turn left (east) on Kootenay Road #3. Follow this road for a few kilometres until you come to a T–intersection, turn right and travel for a short distance to where you will see a road on your left marked Madias Forest Service Road. This is the road that you will be skiing up. Park at the snow line.

Skiing

Ski up the Madias Forest Service Road until you reach the base of a large mountain face at the headwaters of Madias Creek. Skiing is straightforward, but will often involve trail breaking. If you begin skiing at the start of the Madias Road it is approximately 8 km to the end of the valley. The trail generally winds its way through the forest before opening up to views of Indian Head Mountain and its neighbouring peaks. There are several roads that branch off the Madias Road. Stay on the main road (a forestry map would be an asset to have with you). Stay right at the first intersection and left at the next intersection. From here, stay right on the main road and follow it to the valley end.

Be aware that once you reach the end of the valley there is the potential for avalanches off the large alpine faces. Be careful not to expose yourself to the run out zones of these slide paths. There are many safe areas to enjoy the views.

Upper Pedley Bowls. Photo: Chris Hoffstetter.

The Upper Bowls offer exciting ski terrain. Photo: Chris Hofstetter.

Looking west toward Mount Aeneas from the pass. Photo: Chris Hofstetter.

THE PEDLEY BOWLS

The Pedley Bowls offers fantastic ridge touring, multiple wide open alpine bowls, terrific tree skiing in finely spaced larch glades and outstanding views of the Columbia and Kootenay valleys. An unusually abundant snowpack for the Rockies, make this an area not to miss.

Pedley Bowls. Photo: Chris Hoffstetter.

Getting There

From Radium drive south on Highway 93/95 for 12 km to an obvious set of traffic lights at the Invermere turn-off. Proceed straight through the lights for 2.8 km and turn left on the Windermere Loop Road. After 3.2 km turn left then immediately right onto the Westroc Mining Road. Follow to the obvious mine on your right. Park well out of the

way in the plowed area at the end of the road.

From the mine, follow the unplowed road straight ahead of you. When you come to an intersection with three branches, follow the one that goes straight ahead. Continue following this road until you reach the summer parking area. A sign on your right indicates the trailhead. Approximately 10 km from where you park your car. Most parties will spend 1.5 – 2.5 hours to ski up this gently rising road. On your return you can glide most of the way out. It is possible to use a snowmobile to travel to the summer trailhead.

Skiing

A long ridge with an obvious pass intersects the skiing in the Pedley area. To gain this pass, ski past the summer trail marker for a short distance and turn left and follow the obvious creek drainage through the trees until you reach a large open meadow. Cross the meadow towards the steep face at the far end and turn left. Ascend slopes through the trees to gain the ridge. Turn left on the ridge and follow it to the obvious pass. Most parties take approximately one hour to reach the pass from the summer trailhead.

The ridge to the south of the pass gains about 100 vertical metres to an unnamed summit. The views from here on a sunny day are outstanding.

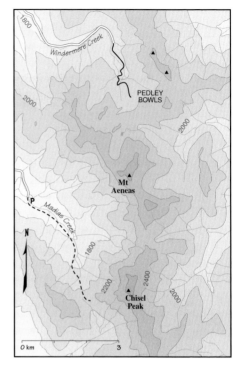

There are several options for ski descents in this area. Four bowls of varying length and steepness can be skied; most involve a mix of tree and alpine terrain.

Another interesting option exists for those who want a longer day, with more demanding terrain. A set of five bowls exists on the far side of the pass. When snow conditions are stable, this area offers steep alpine terrain.

As of time of writing we have heard of less than a dozen people ever to have skied the Pedley Bowls. The terrain and quality of the snow make this one of the premier areas covered in this book.

MOUNT SWANSEA   Touring

The tour up to Mt. Swansea offers fantastic panoramic views of the Columbia Valley. The skiing is up a well-graded road and presents little difficulties but can be a tricky descent if the conditions are icy. An elevation gain of 800 m makes this tour a full days outing for most parties.

Getting There

From Radium travel south on Highway 93/95 for 12 km to the obvious traffic lights, continue for a farther 2.5 km and turn left onto the Windermere Loop Road. Drive straight through the 4-way stop and continue until you see a sign on your left for Mt. Swansea. Turn left and immediately cross the mine hauling road. Park well out of the way of commercial traffic.

Skiing

If there is no snow in the valley, you might want to reconsider doing this tour. January and February are the most reliable times of the year for there to be enough snow covering the road to make it enjoyable.

Begin by skiing up the Mt. Swansea Fire Road. Ski up this road for 5 km until you reach a clearing that is the summer parking lot. A marked trail leaves the far end of the clearing and switchbacks steeply up to the summit. Most parties leave their skis and hike the final 100 m.

There is an outhouse and picnic tables on the summit. During the summer months this is a popular place for paragliding and sight seeing. Descend the same route you came up.

Photo: Ted Johnson.

The Kootenay River is central to many of the trails in the park. Photo: Ted Johnson.

KOOTENAY NATIONAL PARK

Bordering Radium on its west side is the "undiscovered park". Although millions of people travel the highway through Kootenay National Park, few stop to discover this wild place.

We have chosen to describe only the tours in the southern half of the park due to their proximity to town. The skiing in Kootenay offers great views and minimal crowds. Most of the skiing described here is light touring which involves trail–breaking on easy-to-follow trails. The plowed parking areas and a well maintained highway make Kootenay a great place to explore for those who wish to nordic ski away from avalanche danger.

KINDERSLEY PASS

Kindersley Pass offers a mix of skiing through mature forests, sub-alpine and open bowls. A nice one day traverse through beautiful terrain and panoramic scenery. Although the skiing is straightforward, you will be travelling through big avalanche terrain. Best done when you are sure of stable snow conditions. You will need to leave a car on the Kindersley Creek Forestry Service Road if you wish to do the complete traverse. See "Getting Out"

Getting There

From the four way stop in Radium travel east on Highway 93 for 10.6 km to a pull-out on your right. The trail starts directly across the highway in the trees.

Skiing

Start by skiing up through the forest for 3.5 km. Several avalanche paths cross your way, use cautions. Keep following the creek until you break out of treeline. Contour across the north facing slopes. The pass is just off to your right (grid reference 704167).

From the small gap, descend down the north side into Kindersley Creek drainage. Ski for about 1500–1700 vertical feet down the centre of the valley. A road starts part way down the valley on the right side of the creek and will take you back to the Kindersley Forest Road. The descent of this valley offers a nice gentle and long ski through some remote terrain.

Getting Out

If you plan to continue over Kindersly Pass you will need to leave a vehicle as far up the Kindersley Creek Forestry Service Road as you can. From the four way stop in Radium travel north on Highway 95 for 16.5 km and turn right onto Kindersley Creek Forestry Service Road. Depending on snow conditions you may only get a vehicle this far. Drive down this road, there are several side roads but it is quite easy to stay on the main road. Continue past an old historic log flume to where the road splits in two, stay right. Leave your car at snowline.

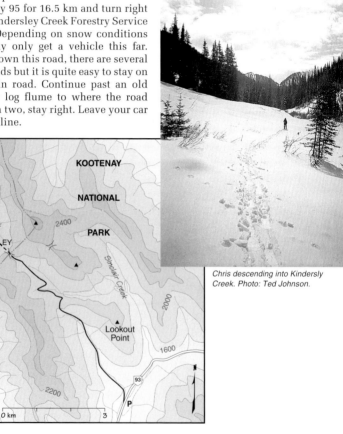

Chris descending into Kindersly Creek. Photo: Ted Johnson.

74

WEST KOOTENAY Touring

The route up the West Kootenay trail is a pleasant way to see Kootenay Park. Skiing is along a relatively flat fire road through a mix of forests with scenic views. Suitable for all levels.

Getting There

From Radium travel north on Highway 93 for 40 km, park at the Kootenay River Warden Station.

Skiing

From the warden station, begin skiing along an old fire road and up a small hill. A short distance later, stay right at a fork in the road. This trail follows the Kootenay River to the park boundary. The views are great, travel is easy and you get a real feeling of being "out there". Return via the same route. The round trip is 26 km and takes most parties a full day.

EAST KOOTENAY Touring

This tour follows an old fireroad and offers a few different options, all of which have nice views of the Kootenay River and surrounding mountains. Suitable for all levels of skiers as either a full or half day tour.

Getting There

From Radium travel north on Highway 93 for 24 km to the McLeod Meadows Picnic Area. The parking lot is usually plowed and there are shelters for day use activities. A nice place to relax after a days exploring.

Skiing

From the Mcleod Meadows picnic area, follow trails through the summer campsites to a suspension bridge over the Kootenay River. From here three options exist. Turn left on the fire road and you can travel for 7 km to Daer Creek. Turn right on the fire road and follow for 5 km to Pitts Creek. By continuing straight ahead you can follow the signs to a loop through Dog Lake for 5 km. All tours are easy to follow and present little difficulties.

This scenic suspension bridge leads to Dog Lake.
Photo: Ted Johnson.

A rustic shelter in Kootenay National Park.

HECTOR GORGE   Touring

An enjoyable half day trip along an easy to follow fire road. A panoramic backdrop of stunning peaks makes this tour worthwhile. Suitable for all skill levels.

Getting There

From Radium travel north on Highway 93 to 1.8 km past the Dolly Varden Winter Campsite. Park on the east side of the highway. Shuttle a vehicle further up the highway to the trails end, at the Hector Gorge lookout. The trail joins the highway 0.5 km before the parking area.

Skiing

Cross the gate on the old fire road and follow over a bridge across the Kootenay River. Just before you reach a second bridge, turn left and follow the obvious route to your awaiting vehicle. A distance of 9 km, with little elevation gain makes for a nice afternoon.

DOLLY VARDEN

This tour offers straightforward skiing on an easy to follow route with great views and a sense of remoteness. Used in conjunction with the West Kootenay Trail, this route can make for a very fulfilling day. The option of travelling one way with a car shuttle or returning the way you came depending on how long a day you want, makes this tour perfect for all levels of skiers.

Getting There

From Radium travel north on Highway 93 for 33 km to the gate to Crooks Meadow on the west (left) side of the road. A farther 7 km will bring you to the Kootenay River Wardens Station.

Skiing

From the gate to Crooks Meadow ski through the open clearing and pick up

the West Kootenay Fire Road and follow it for 10 km to a junction in the trail. Stay right and descend a small hill into the Kootenay River Warden Station. Either return the way you came or exit to your awaiting vehicle. There is little elevation gain and the route is easy to follow, suitable for all levels of skiers.

Early season snow on the Dolly Varden trail.
Photo: Ted Johnson.

77

Backcountry Huts, Cabins & Lodges

BACKCOUNTRY HUTS, CABINS AND LODGES

One of the great attributes of the mountains in this area, is the available accommodation in the backcountry. There are many places to stay, from first class lodges to questionable shelters. There are several cabins that we have not included in this book due to the fact that they are located either on private land, or land that has been leased from the government.

There are two cabins owned by the Windermere Snowmobile Society in the area. We have listed these as emergency shelters because they were not built with skiers in mind, and are used frequently by the snowmobile crowd. If you are planning to use these cabins as a day shelter, you are required to purchase a yearly membership from the Windermere Valley Snowmobile Society.

The firewood provided for all of these locations was brought there at considerable expense, please use it sparingly. In several locations the wood has to be brought in by helicopter and, once the wood is used up, there is no more for the season.

We ask you to leave the cabins and surrounding areas cleaner than when you showed up. Clean your dishes; sweep the floor and pack out all of your garbage, and that left by others before you. It only takes a few minutes to do these small chores and makes a big difference to the next group using the facilities.

Almost all of the accommodations provided have some sort of bathroom facility. Use it! There is nothing worse than showing up at a cabin and finding human waste strewn about to spoil one of these scenic locations. If you can't locate the facilities, which can be the case in a big snow year, have your group use one location at least 50 m away from the cabin and far away from any source of drinking water or watershed.

Locals built most of the cabins listed here at their own personal time and expense. We urge you to treat them with the respect they deserve.

The Conrad Kain hut (circled) is barely visible below Snowpatch Spire. Photo: Ted Johnson.

CONRAD KAIN HUT

The "Kain Hut" in the Bugaboos was originally built in 1972, by the Alpine Club of Canada in honour of legendary mountaineer, Conrad Kain. Kain was an Austrian born mountain guide who was among the original party of explorers to first visit this area in 1910. He achieved many outstanding ascents around here. The hut sits at an elevation of 2170 m and is located at GR 166204. The Alpine Club of Canada maintains the hut and can be reached by phone at (403) 678-3200. Reservations should be made in advance, although there is lots of room for several parties. Until March 1st there is no charge for the hut. After March 1st there is a cost of $21.00 per person per night. You should contact B.C. Parks at (250) 244-3212 and advise them of your length of stay, number of people in party, and your mode of access into the park.

Hut amenities include sleeping room for up to fifty people. Sleeping pads are provided. During winter you will want to bring your own stoves, pots and fuel, as they are not provided. The Kain Hut can be a cold place to stay, as there is no source of heat, it is recommended to plan your visit during warm, clear weather.

Approaching the Conrad Kain Hut in late spring conditions. Photo: Jeff Haack.

Photo: Ted Johnson.

FORESTER SNOWMOBILE CABIN

The Forester Snowmobile Cabin is located in the Forester Basin at the end of the groomed snowmobile trail. It is owned and maintained by the Windermere Valley Snowmobile Society. Classified as an emergency shelter, the "Sled Shed" is conveniently located if things go wrong.

The cabin is equipped with a barbecue, wood stove and a generator. The "Sled Shed" was built in the summer of 2000 and is easy to find, and makes for a cozy place to get out of the elements. A lot of snowmobile traffic can make the cabin crowded and it should only be used by skiers in an emergency.

DAVE WHYTE HUT

Built in 2001 as a memorial to a young local skier who was tragically killed in an avalanche, the Dave Whyte Hut is a fantastic place to spend a few days. The tremendous skiing in the area, combined with the other nearby huts make this a great starting point for a trip to the Forester area.

If it is your first time in the area, it can be a bit challenging to find the hut if the visibility is bad. The hut is located approximately half way down the Forester Basin, on the righthand (north) side, and is situated about 30 m above the valley floor, tucked away in the trees. A good landmark to use is the wide open face just to the west of the trees that hide the cabin. Most parties gain the cabin up a non-distinct creek bed just below the hut.

If you are having trouble locating the hut, one option is to travel down the south side of the basin scanning the trees on the opposite side. The hut is visible just above the valley floor in a very small opening in the trees. Grid reference N 50:39.888 W 116:32.725

The Dave Whyte Hut sleeps 4 comfortably and is equipped with sleeping mats, a Coleman stove, a wood stove, kitchen utensils and dishes. From the stainless steel counters to the quality construction, this hut is like a home away from home.

Owned by the Windermere Hut Society, the Dave Whyte Hut can be booked by calling Copies, Boxes Etc. in Invermere at 250-342-5005. Reservations can be made 60 days in advance and we recommend calling early as it tends to fill up quickly.

Photo: Ted Johnson.

OLIVE HUT

The Olive Hut is situated on a rock outcropping on the edge of the Catamount Glacier, and offers outstanding scenery, comfortable accommodations and amazing ski touring. The hut can sleep up to 6 people and is equipped with a Coleman stove, wood stove, pots, dishes and cooking utensils.

Located on the east side of the Scotch Peaks on a rock fin just off the Catamount glacier (GR 313088), the Olive Hut is ideally situated for ski touring. In bad visibility it can be extremely difficult to find and you might want to consider one of the huts in the Forester Basin until the weather clears.

Reservations can be made 60 days in advance by calling Copies Boxes Etc. at 250-342-5005. The hut is owned by the Windermere Valley Hut Society and there is a charge of $10 per night per person. The hut was named after Peter and Debbie Olive who were tragically killed in a helicopter accident.

PARADISE SNOWMOBILE CABIN

Located at the terminus of the groomed snowmobile trail to Paradise Bowl, this cabin is ideally situated as an emergency shelter.

This cabin is owned by the Windermere Valley Snowmobile Club and maintained by Toby Creek Adventures. Equipped with a wood stove and barbecue, this cabin is a great place to be if you have an emergency.

This cabin was once part of the original mining town of Paradise Town around the turn of the century and was part of a large town and mine site where almost 100 people used to live year round. The cabin has under gone extensive repairs and facelifts over the years and can almost be considered a "new" cabin.

This cabin is used by Toby Creek Adventures for their commercial snowmobile tours on a daily basis and by the general public as a warming hut.

Photo: Ted Johnson.

Photo: Ted Johnson.

JUMBO PASS CABIN

The Jumbo Cabin is an excellent place to have a ski holiday. The cabin is comfortable, and the skiing is fantastic. This cabin was rebuilt in 1998 and offers room for 6-8 people to sleep. The cabin is owned by the Windermere Valley Hut Society and can be booked by calling Copies, Boxes, Etc. at 250-342-5005. The cost of the cabin is $10 per person per night. You can book the whole cabin for your party at a cost of $60 per night. Reservations can be made 60 days in advance and it is not recommended that you wait to the last minute to book your trip, as this area is extremely popular and tends to fill up fast.

The cabin is equipped with sleeping mats, a coleman stove, a wood stove and firewood.

Photo, courtesy Nipika Lodge.

NIPIKA LODGE

The lodge and cabins at the Nipika Touring Centre provide superb log construction accommodations at a reasonable price. Combined with their facilities and ski trails, Nipika is a wonderful destination for a nordic ski holiday.

The main lodge has accommodations for 13 people and a spacious main floor with a restaurant serving three meals daily. A cozy wood burning fireplace, with ample room to laze about, makes this a great après ski area.

A variety of private cabins are available for those wishing a little more privacy. Accommodating from 4 to 10 people, these cabins are equipped with full kitchens and private bathrooms.

Nipika offers more than just great accommodations and nordic skiing. A hot tub/sauna facility, an outdoor skating rink (skates available), a ski repair and waxing area, snowshoe trails, and ski trails right to your door let Nipika offer everything you could want in a ski destination.

Rates are $80 per person/per night with discounts for children and in the off season. For more information call 250-342-6516 or online at Nipika.com.

THE AUTHORS

Ted Johnson

Ted grew up in Europe and started skiing in 1975. He spent his school years in Ontario, with weekends spent skiing in the Laurentian Mountains of Quebec. He switched to snowboarding in 1988 and hasn't looked back since.

Ted moved to western Canada in 1993, making a living guiding on the rivers and in the mountains of B.C. and Alberta. He has been exploring the backcountry ever since. Armed with a snowmobile and a splitboard, he is one of a new breed of mountain explorer.

Chris Hofstetter

Chris was born in Ontario and moved to Western Canada in 1978. Chris started skiing with his family at the age of five.

Once he was done with his schooling skiing became his main focus and he started ski tour guiding throughout the Canadian Rockies and the interior of British Columbia. Since then Chris has spent many years skiing and climbing throughout North America and in New Zealand. Radium Hot Springs has always been where Chris chooses to call home.

USEFULL PHONE NUMBERS

RCMP Invermere	250-342-9292
Warden Service Emergency (Banff)	403-762-4506
Kootenay National Park Information	250-347-9361
Kool Country Towing	250-342-4400
Towing (Radium Esso)	250-347-9726
Radium Chamber of Commerce	250-347-9331

Snowmobile Rentals and Shuttles

Motor Tech Skidoo Dealership	250-344-2888
Toby Creek Adventures	250-342-5047

Backcountry Equipment Rentals

Calgary University Outdoor Rentals	403-220-5038

Our recomdations in for accomodation in Radium

Ritz Motel (Good clean family run motel)	250-347-9644
Invermere International Hostel	250-342-3445
Misty River Lodge (Radium)	250-347-9912

Avalanche Hazard and Snow Stability

Public Avalanche Information Bulletin (Canadian Avalanche Association)
1-800-667-1105 or www.avalanche.ca

Note: the toll free number is not accessible from the USA

Banff/Kootenay/Yoho Parks Avalanche Bulletin 403-762-1460

Visit our website at
www.rmbooks.com